Lyme Disease Cookbook

MAIN COURSE – Effective recipes designed to treat chronic inflammation with specific nutritional information's (Proven recipes to treat lyme disease)

TABLE OF CONTENTS

BREAKFAST 7

CHOCOLATE COCONUT OATS 7

QUINOA MUESLY WITH COCONUT MILK 8

SWEET POTATO 9

BANANA SPLIT 10

CHAI-SPICED PEAR OATMEAL 11

CHOCOLATE BREAD 13

COCONUT CRACKERS 14

ALMOND BUTTER 16

LEMON ZINGER BARS 17

SEED CRACKERS 19

SWEET POTATO FLATBREAD 20

MANGO BEET SALAD 22

OATMEAL SQUARES WITH MULBERRIES 23

SESAME ALMOND COOKIES 25

GLUTEN-FREE OATMEAL 26

QUINOA CRANBERRY SALAD 27

BLACK BEAN AND TAAHINI DIP 28

CHIA LEMON QUINOA 29

GLUTEN-FREE QUINOA SWEET-PEA SALAD 30

BUTTERNUT SQUASH WITH ALMOND BUTTER 31

LUNCH 32

EGG SALAD 32

PICKLED BEETS 33

AVOCADO DIP 34

- VANILLA ALMOND BLAST 35
- EGGS WITH BEARNAISE SAUCE 36
- GREEN BEANS WITH MUSHROOMS 37
- STEAMED VEGETABLES 39
- SCRAMBLED EGGS WITH MUSHROOMS 40
- COCONUT ALMOND COOKIE 41
- ASPARAGUS SOUP 42
- RICE PANCAKE 44
- ALMOND TIPALIA 45
- ARTICHOKE LEK SOUP 46
- COCONUT SMOOTHIE 47
- ALMOND BUTTER 48
- BROILED FLOUNDER 49
- CINNAMON APPLESAUCE 50
- SHREDDED CARROT SALAD 51
- MOROCCAN SALMON 52
- GRILLED SALMON WITH HERB VINAIGRETTE 54
- **DINNER** 56
- BAKED ZUCCHINI 56
- GREEN CHILE RICE 57
- PESTO 58
- SWEET TOMATO RELISH 59
- MACARONI AND CHEESE 60
- ROASTED BRUSEELS SPROUTS 62
- CARAMELIZED ONION AND BACON 63
- CORNCAKE 64

TERIYAKI BURGER	65
BBQ CHICKEN SALAD	66
STRAWBERRY SALAD	67
CHICKEN PASTA SALAD	68
SPINACH PASTA SALAD	69
BUTTERNUT SQUASH SOUP	71
TACO SOUP	72
PUMPKIN CHILI	73
CHICKEN PIE SOUP	75
TOMATO TORTELLINI SOUP	77
MASHED SWEET POTATO SOUP	79
TURKEY SOUP	80
DESSERT	**82**
GRANOLA COOKIES	82
COCONUT OIL CHEX MIX	83
CHOCOLATE COCONUT COOKIE	84
COCONUT OIL CRISPY TREATS	85
PEANUT BUTTER BALLS	86
COCONUT OIL BROWNIES	87
BLUEBERRY BANANA MUFFINS	89
COCONUT OIL COOKIES	91
GLUTEN FREE INSTANT POT OATMEAL	92
BANANA BREAD COOKIES	93
CHOCOLATE BALLS	95
ORANGE CREAMSICLE BALLS	96
PEANUT BUTTER COCONUT BITES	97

CARROT CAKE BITES 98

PEACH COBBLER SMOOTHIE 99

CHERRY COCONUT SMOOTHIE.. 100

COCONUT BLACKOUT SMOOTHIE 101

CARROT TURMERIC SMOTHEI 102

GINGERBREAD SMOOTHIE 103

SWEET POTATO SMOOTHIE 104

Copyright 2018 by Noah Jerris - All rights reserved.

This document is geared towards providing exact and reliable information in regards to the topic and issue covered. The publication is sold with the idea that the publisher is not required to render accounting, officially permitted, or otherwise, qualified services. If advice is necessary, legal or professional, a practiced individual in the profession should be ordered.

- From a Declaration of Principles which was accepted and approved equally by a Committee of the American Bar Association and a Committee of Publishers and Associations.

In no way is it legal to reproduce, duplicate, or transmit any part of this document in either electronic means or in printed format. Recording of this publication is strictly prohibited and any storage of this document is not allowed unless with written permission from the publisher. All rights reserved.

The information provided herein is stated to be truthful and consistent, in that any liability, in terms of inattention or otherwise, by any usage or abuse of any policies, processes, or directions contained within is the solitary and utter responsibility of the recipient reader. Under no circumstances will any legal responsibility or blame be held against the publisher for any reparation, damages, or monetary loss due to the information herein, either directly or indirectly.

Respective authors own all copyrights not held by the publisher.

The information herein is offered for informational purposes solely, and is universal as so. The presentation of the information is without contract or any type of guarantee assurance.

The trademarks that are used are without any consent, and the publication of the trademark is without permission or backing by the trademark owner. All trademarks and brands within this book are for clarifying purposes only and are the owned by the owners themselves, not affiliated with this document.

Introduction

Lyme disease recipes for borrelia problems but also for family enjoyment. You will love them for sure for how easy it is to prepare them.

BREAKFAST

CHOCOLATE COCONUT OATS

Serves: 4
Prep Time: 10 Minutes
Cook Time: 10 Minutes
Total Time: 20 Minutes

INGREDIENTS

- 1 cup oats
- 2 tablespoons chia seeds
- 2 tablespoons maple syrup
- 1 vanilla extract
- 1 tablespoons cocoa powder
- 1 cup water
- 2/3 cup coconut milk
- 2 tablespoons water

DIRECTIONS

1. In a bowl mix oat with water and place it in the fridge overnight
2. In the morning add chia seeds and coconut milk
3. Transfer mixture to a skillet and cook for 5 minutes

4. Remove and move into serving bowl and add vanilla extract, cacao powder and maple syrup
5. Serve when ready

QUINOA MUESLY WITH COCONUT MILK

Serves: *4*

Prep Time: *10* Minutes

Cook Time: *10* Minutes

Total Time: *20* Minutes

INGREDIENTS

- 1 cup Quinoa
- ½ cup coconut milk yogurt
- 1 pinch ground cinnamon
- 1 cup Grain Free Muesli

DIRECTIONS

1. Cook the quinoa according to the indications, nd set aside
2. Drizzle the quinoa with coconut milk yogurt and top with grain free muesli
3. Add cinnamon to each bowl and serve

SWEET POTATO

Serves: **4**

Prep Time: **10** Minutes

Cook Time: **30** Minutes

Total Time: **40** Minutes

INGREDIENTS

- 3 sweet potatoes
- 8 tablespoons almond milk
- 1 tablespoon mint leaves
- 1 tablespoon lemon zest
- 1 tablespoon coconut oil
- 1 pinch salt
- 1 pinch ground cinnamon
- 3 tablespoons vanilla cereal

DIRECTIONS

1. Preheat oven to 350 F and line a baking sheet with parchment paper
2. Place the sweet potatoes on the baking sheet
3. Rub the sweet potato with coconut oil and sprinkle salt and pepper
4. Roast for 30 minutes

5. Remove the sweet potatoes from the oven and cut into small pieces
6. Top with coconut oil, lemon zest and cereal mixture

BANANA SPLIT

Serves: 2

Prep Time: 10 Minutes

Cook Time: 10 Minutes

Total Time: 20 Minutes

INGREDIENTS

- 2 bananas
- 1 cup strawberries
- 1 cup blackberries
- 1 cup chopped pineapple
- 1 cup coconut milk
- 1 tablespoon whole grain granola
- ¼ ounce roasted coconut chips

DIRECTIONS

1. Slice the bananas and place them into a bowl
2. Divide the strawberries, blackberries and pineapple and place it in the bottom of the bowl

3. Top with yogurt and divide the granola and coconut chips between the bananas

CHAI-SPICED PEAR OATMEAL

Serves: 2

Prep Time: 10 Minutes

Cook Time: 30 Minutes

Total Time: 40 Minutes

INGREDIENTS

- 1 cup oats
- ½ tsp ground cinnamon
- 1 tsp maple syrup
- 1 tablespoon walnut halves
- 2 tsp coconut oil
- 1 Anjou pear spiralized with blade
- 1 cup almond milk
- ½ tsp vanilla extract

DIRECTIONS

1. In a saucepan boil water and add oats for another 10 minutes

2. In a skillet heat coconut oil over medium heat and add almond milk, pear noodles, cinnamon, maple syrup and vanilla extract
3. Stir to simmer for about 10-15 minutes
    4. In another skillet place walnuts and cook for 5-6 minutes, remove from pan when ready
    5. Place the oatmeal in a bowl and top with pear mixture and toasted walnuts

CHOCOLATE BREAD

Serves: **2**

Prep Time: **10** Minutes

Cook Time: **30** Minutes

Total Time: **40** Minutes

INGREDIENTS

- Coconut oil
- 1 cup oat flour
- ½ cup almond flour
- 1 tablespoon flaxseeds
- 5 tablespoons water
- ½ cup almond milk
- 1 tsp baking powder
- 1 tsp baking soda
- 1 tsp vanilla extract
- ½ cup maple syrup
- 1 banana
- ½ cup cocoa powder

DIRECTIONS

1. **Preheat oven to 300 F**
2. **Mix water with flax and water and set aside**

3. In a bowl mash the banana and add remaining ingredients
4. Transfer the mixture to a loaf pan and bake for 40 minutes
5. Remove from the oven and let it cool
6. Slice the bread and serve

COCONUT CRACKERS

Serves: 2

Prep Time: 10 Minutes

Cook Time: 60 Minutes

Total Time: 70 Minutes

INGREDIENTS

- 1 cup hazelnut flour
- 1 peach
- 8 tablespoons water
- 6 tablespoons olive oil
- ¾ tsp salt
- 1 tsp cacao powder
- ½ tsp cinnamon
- 1 cup water
- ¼ tsp ginger
- ½ tablespoons coconut flakes

- 1 cup coconut flour
- 2 tablespoons flaxseeds
- 1 tablespoon cherries

DIRECTIONS

1. Preheat oven to 325 F
2. In a bowl mix water with flaxseeds
3. In another bowl mix all the ingredients, excepting coconut flakes and form a ball
4. Transfer the dough to a baking sheet with parchment paper
5. Sprinkle with coconut flakes and bake for 50 minutes
6. Remove and let it cool before serving

ALMOND BUTTER

Serves: **4**

Prep Time: **10** Minutes

Cook Time: **30** Minutes

Total Time: **40** Minutes

INGREDIENTS

- 1 cup pitted dates
- 2 bananas
- 1 cup almond flour
- 1 cup oats
- 2 tablespoons almond butter
- 2 tablespoons cherries
- 1 tsp sesame seeds

DIRECTIONS

1. In a food processor puree the dates until well combined
2. Add bananas and puree them also
3. Add oats, almond butter, almond flour, and puree until well combined
4. Transfer to the fridge for 25-30 minutes
5. Remove from fridge and add cherries and mix and also sesame seeds

6. Roll into small balls and place them on a baking sheet and bake for 20-25 minutes
7. Remove from oven and let them cool before serving

LEMON ZINGER BARS

Serves: 4
Prep Time: 15 Minutes
Cook Time: 35 Minutes
Total Time: 50 Minutes

INGREDIENTS

- 2 cups oats
- zest from 2 lemons
- 2/4 cup water
- 3 pitted dates chopped
- 2/4 cup apricots

DIRECTIONS

1. Preheat oven to 350 F
2. In a food processor add the oats and blend, pour the mixture into a bowl
3. Add the dates and apricots to the food processor

4. Add water and lemon juice and blend, let the mixture rest for 25-30 minutes
5. Bake for 30-35 minutes until golden brown and then remove from the oven
6. Remove from the pan onto a cutting board and cut into small bars
7. Store in a container for 1 week

SEED CRACKERS

Serves: *4*

Prep Time: *10* Minutes

Cook Time: *20* Minutes

Total Time: *30* Minutes

INGREDIENTS

- ¾ cup pumpkin seeds
- 1 tablespoon hemp seeds
- 1 tsp sesame seeds
- ¼ cup carrot
- 1 tsp parsley
- ¼ tsp Chile powder
- 1/8 garlic
- ¼ tsp salt
- 1 tablespoons water
- ½ cup sunflower seeds

DIRECTIONS

1. Preheat oven to 325 F
2. In a blender place all the ingredients and blend
3. Add water and blend until a rough dough forms
4. Place the dough on a parchment paper

5. Use a pizza cutter to trim the edges and transfer to the oven
6. Bake for 15-20 minutes and remove from oven
7. Let it cool and serve

SWEET POTATO FLATBREAD

Serves: 4

Prep Time: 25 Minutes

Cook Time: 45 Minutes

Total Time: 70 Minutes

INGREDIENTS

- 1 sweet potato
- 2 tablespoons olive oil
- 1 tablespoon flaxseeds
- 2 tablespoons water
- 2 cups almond flour
- 1 tsp thyme
- 1 tsp chopped rosemary
- ½ tsp sea salt

DIRECTIONS

1. Preheat the oven to 325 F

2. Steam the sweet potato in a steamer basket over medium heat
3. In a bowl mix water with flaxseeds and set aside
4. In a bowl mash the sweet potatoes and add the remaining ingredients and mix
5. Transfer the mixture to a parchment lined baking sheet
6. Bake for 40 minutes or until golden brown
7. Remove from the oven and let it cool before serving

MANGO BEET SALAD

Serves: **4**

Prep Time: **20** Minutes

Cook Time: **40** Minutes

Total Time: **60** Minutes

INGREDIENTS

- 5 beets
- 1 mango peeled
- 2 tablespoons walnuts
- 1 tablespoon coconut flakes
- 1 cup arugula
- 1 tablespoon almond oil
- juice from 1 lemon
- 1 pinch of salt

DIRECTIONS

1. Preheat the oven to 375 F
2. In a baking dish add the beets and roast for 35 minutes and add water, remove set aside
3. In another bowl mix the mango, walnuts, beets, arugula and coconut flakes
4. In a small bowl whisk lemon juice, sea salt, pepper, almond oil, pepper and salt

5. Drizzle the dressing over the salad and serve

OATMEAL SQUARES WITH MULBERRIES

Serves: *4*
Prep Time: *10* Minutes
Cook Time: *30* Minutes
Total Time: *40* Minutes

INGREDIENTS

- Coconut oil
- 1 cup coconut milk
- 1 tablespoons vanilla extract
- 1 tablespoon maple syrup
- 1 cup while mulberries
- ½ tsp ground cinnamon
- 2 cups oats
- 2 tablespoons flaxseeds
- ¼ tsp salt
- ¼ tsp pumpkin pie spice
- ¼ tsp ground ginger

DIRECTIONS

1. Preheat oven to 325 F and grease a baking dish with coconut oil
2. Mix all the ingredients except cinnamon and transfer to a baking dish and sprinkle with cinnamon
3. Bake for 25-30 minutes, remove and let it cool
4. Cut into squares and serve

SESAME ALMOND COOKIES

Serves: **4**

Prep Time: **10** Minutes

Cook Time: **20** Minutes

Total Time: **30** Minutes

INGREDIENTS

- 2 cups almond flour
- 2 tablespoons maple syrup
- 1 tablespoon coconut oil
- 3 tablespoons flaxseeds
- ½ tsp baking soda
- 1 tablespoon sesame seeds
- black pepper
- 1 pinch salt
- 1 pinch cinnamon

DIRECTIONS

1. Preheat oven to 325 F
2. In a bowl mix baking soda, almond flour, flaxseeds, sea salt and black pepper until well combined
3. Add coconut oil, maple syrup and vanilla extract and mix well
4. Add sesame seeds and cinnamon

5. Transfer to baking sheets by forming small cookies
6. Bake for 15-20 minutes and remove
7. Let it cool before serving

GLUTEN-FREE OATMEAL

Serves: *1*

Prep Time: *5* Minutes

Cook Time: *10* Minutes

Total Time: *15* Minutes

INGREDIENTS

- 1/3 cup gluten free oats
- nourish snacks mocha mazing
- nourish snacks nutty nanas

DIRECTIONS

1. Cook oats following the indications on the package
2. Add almond milk with topping and serve

QUINOA CRANBERRY SALAD

Serves: *2*

Prep Time: *10* Minutes

Cook Time: *10* Minutes

Total Time: *20* Minutes

INGREDIENTS

- 1 cup quinoa
- 1 tablespoons cashews
- 1 tablespoon fresh basil
- 1 tablespoon vinegar
- 1 tablespoon olive oil
- 1 tsp orange juice
- ½ orange zest
- salt
- 1 red pepper
- 2 tablespoons cranberries

DIRECTIONS

1. Cook quinoa following the indications on the package
2. In a bowl toss quinoa with pepper, cashews, cranberries and basil
3. In another bowl whisk orange zest, salt, olive oil, vinegar, pepper and drizzle over quinoa salad

BLACK BEAN AND TAAHINI DIP

Serves: *1*

Prep Time: *5* Minutes

Cook Time: *5* Minutes

Total Time: *10* Minutes

INGREDIENTS

- 1 15 oz. black beans
- 1 tsp flax seeds
- sea salt
- ½ cup tahini sesame seeds

DIRECTIONS

1. In a food processor add all the ingredients and puree until smooth
2. Transfer to a bowl and serve

CHIA LEMON QUINOA

Serves: **2**

Prep Time: **10** Minutes

Cook Time: **10** Minutes

Total Time: **20** Minutes

INGREDIENTS

- 1 cup quinoa
- 4 tablespoons maple syrup
- 3 tablespoons almonds
- 1 tablespoon chia seeds
- ½ tsp salt
- lemon zest
- 1 cup almond milk

DIRECTIONS

1. Cook quinoa following the indications on the package
2. Remove from heat and set aside
3. Add maple syrup, honey, chia seeds, almond milk, lemon zest and serve

GLUTEN-FREE QUINOA SWEET-PEA SALAD

Serves: **3**

Prep Time: **10** Minutes

Cook Time: **10** Minutes

Total Time: **20** Minutes

INGREDIENTS

- ½ cup quinoa
- 2 tablespoons parsley
- ¼ tsp orange zest
- ¼ tsp salt
- 1 bottle gluten-free beer
- 1/3 tsp cumin
- 2 tablespoons olive oil
- 1 red bell pepper

DIRECTIONS

1. Cook quinoa following the indications on the package
2. Remove and transfer to a bowl and set aside
3. Add the remaining ingredients and toss
4. Serve when ready

BUTTERNUT SQUASH WITH ALMOND BUTTER

Serves: *3*

Prep Time: *10* Minutes

Cook Time: *60* Minutes

Total Time: *70* Minutes

INGREDIENTS

- 2 tablespoons almond butter
- 1 butternut squash
- 1 pinch salt
- 1 pinch lemon zest

DIRECTIONS

1. **Preheat oven to 325 F**
2. **In a baking dish place the squash and sprinkle with salt**
3. **Pour water into the baking dish and bake for 60 minutes**
4. **Remove from oven and drizzle with almond butter and lemon zest**
5. **Season with salt and pepper before serving**

LUNCH

EGG SALAD

Serves: 2

Prep Time: 10 Minutes

Cook Time: 20 Minutes

Total Time: 30 Minutes

INGREDIENTS

- 5 eggs boiled and peeled
- 1 tablespoon mustard
- ½ tsp salt
- 2 tablespoons mayonnaise

DIRECTIONS

1. Cut the eggs in half and remove the yolks
2. In a bowl add all the ingredients and the yolks and mix everything
3. Spoon the mixture into the egg whites and serve

PICKLED BEETS

Serves: *4*

Prep Time: *10* Minutes

Cook Time: *60* Minutes

Total Time: *70* Minutes

INGREDIENTS

- 1 bunch beets
- ¼ cup cider vinegar
- ¼ cup water
- 1 onion
- 1 clove garlic
- ¼ tsp salt
- 1 tablespoon honey

DIRECTIONS

1. In a saucepan add the beets and water and boil on high heat for 40-45 minutes
2. Drain and peel the beets and slice them
3. Put the beets back in the saucepan and add the rest of the ingredients except honey
4. Cook for 10-15 minutes
5. Remove from heat and add honey

AVOCADO DIP

Serves: 2
Prep Time: 5 Minutes
Cook Time: 10 Minutes
Total Time: 15 Minutes

INGREDIENTS

- 2 avocados
- ¼ cup mayonnaise
- ¼ tsp salt
- ½ tsp sesame oil
- 1 clove garlic
- 1 tablespoon chives

DIRECTIONS

1. Place all the ingredients in a blender and blend until smooth
2. Remove and serve

VANILLA ALMOND BLAST

Serves: 2

Prep Time: 10 Minutes

Cook Time: 5 Minutes

Total Time: 15 Minutes

INGREDIENTS

- 1 cup frozen cherries
- ¼ tsp almond extract
- 1 tsp honey
- ¼ cup ice cubes
- 1 tsp flaxseed
- ¾ cup almond milk
- ¼ tsp vanilla

DIRECTIONS

1. In a blender add all the ingredients and blend until smooth
2. Pour into a glass and serve

EGGS WITH BEARNAISE SAUCE

Serves: **3**

Prep Time: **20** Minutes

Cook Time: **20** Minutes

Total Time: **40** Minutes

INGREDIENTS

- 1 serving béarnaise sauce
- 2 cups water
- 3 eggs
- 1 tsp apple cider vinegar
- parsley
- 1 tablespoon ghee
- 1 shallot
- 1 clove garlic
- 1 lbs. baby spinach

DIRECTIONS

1. Prepare the sauce and set aside
2. In a pan heat the ghee and add garlic, shallot and sauté over medium heat
3. Add spinach and water and boil for 4-5 minutes and add vinegar when water is boiling
4. In a custard cup crack the eggs

5. Add the eggs and poach for 2-3 minutes
6. Divide the spinach on 3 plates and top with eggs

GREEN BEANS WITH MUSHROOMS

Serves: **4**

Prep Time: **10** Minutes

Cook Time: **10** Minutes

Total Time: **20** Minutes

INGREDIENTS

- ½ lbs. green beans
- 1 shallot
- ¼ tsp thyme leaves
- ¼ tsp basil
- 1 tsp cider vinegar
- 1 clove garlic
- 3-ounces mushrooms
- ¼ tsp salt
- 1 tablespoon almonds
- 1 tablespoon olive oil

DIRECTIONS

1. Steam the beans for 4-5 minutes
2. In a pan add olive oil and shallot and sauce over medium heat for 2-3 minutes
3. Add garlic, mushrooms and green beans and sauté for 2-3 minutes
4. Stir in thyme, salt, basil and vinegar
5. Sprinkle sliced almonds over and serve

STEAMED VEGETABLES

Serves: *4*

Prep Time: *10* Minutes

Cook Time: *20* Minutes

Total Time: *30* Minutes

INGREDIENTS

- 2 cups cooked brown rice
- 2 ounces steamed green beans
- 1 cup bok choy
- 1 cup carrots

DIRECTIONS

1. On a plate place the rice and top with green beans, carrots and bok choy
2. Spoon vinaigrette over the vegetables and serve

SCRAMBLED EGGS WITH MUSHROOMS

Serves: *3*

Prep Time: *10* Minutes

Cook Time: *10* Minutes

Total Time: *20* Minutes

INGREDIENTS

- 1 tsp olive oil
- 1 cup mushrooms
- 1 scallion
- 1 clove of garlic
- 1 tsp chopped herbs
- ¼ tsp salt
- 1 egg beaten

DIRECTIONS

1. In a pan add garlic, mushrooms and scallion over medium heat and cook for 2-3 minutes
2. Mix the egg with the herbs and pour the mixture into the pan
3. Cook for another 3-4 minutes

COCONUT ALMOND COOKIE

Serves: 3

Prep Time: 10 Minutes

Cook Time: 10 Minutes

Total Time: 20 Minutes

INGREDIENTS

- 1 cup almond flour
- ½ cup coconut
- 1 tablespoon honey
- 1 tablespoon coconut oil
- 1 tsp vanilla extract
- ¼ tsp almond extract
- 1 pinch salt

DIRECTIONS

1. Preheat oven to 325 F
2. Place all the ingredients in a blender and blend until smooth
3. Line a baking sheet with parchment paper and divide the dough into 9 portions
4. Bake for 10 minutes or until brown, remove and serve

ASPARAGUS SOUP

Serves: **4**

Prep Time: **10** Minutes

Cook Time: **45** Minutes

Total Time: **55** Minutes

INGREDIENTS

- 2 tablespoons olive oil
- 1 tsp salt
- 2 cups vegetable broth
- 1 stalk celery
- 6 oz. asparagus
- 1 tsp chopped dill
- 1 cup coconut milk
- 1 onion
- 1 clove garlic
- 1 carrot
- ¼ tsp chopped parsley

DIRECTIONS

1. In a saucepan add onions and sauté for 2-3 minutes over medium heat
2. Add asparagus, garlic, carrots and sauté for another 4-5 minutes

3. Add the remaining ingredients and bring to boil for 30-34 minutes
4. Remove from heat and let it cool
5. Puree the soup until smooth and serve

RICE PANCAKE

Serves: **4**

Prep Time: **10** Minutes

Cook Time: **30** Minutes

Total Time: **40** Minutes

INGREDIENTS

- 1 tablespoon olive oil
- ¼ tsp salt
- ¼ tsp garlic powder
- 1 egg
- 1 cup brown rice
- 1 tsp chopped parsley
- 1 tsp chopped chives

DIRECTIONS

1. **In a bowl mix all the ingredients**
2. **Pour the mixture into a frying pan over medium heat**
3. **Cook for 4-5 minutes**
4. **Remove and serve**

ALMOND TIPALIA

Serves: 2
Prep Time: 10 Minutes
Cook Time: 10 Minutes
Total Time: 20 Minutes

INGREDIENTS

- 2/3 cup almond meal
- 4 tilapia filets
- 2 tablespoons coconut oil
- 1 tsp chopped parsley
- 1 clove garlic
- ½ tsp salt

DIRECTIONS

1. In a bowl mix herbs, salt and garlic
2. Coat both side of filet with the mixture
3. Refrigerate the fish for 30-40 minutes
4. Heat oil in a frying pan and cook the fish 5-6 minutes per side

ARTICHOKE LEK SOUP

Serves: **4**

Prep Time: **10** Minutes

Cook Time: **20** Minutes

Total Time: **30** Minutes

INGREDIENTS

- 1 tablespoon olive oil
- ½ cup almond milk
- ¼ tsp salt
- 1 tsp parsley
- 2 leeks
- 2 cloves garlic
- 1 can artichoke hearts
- 1 cup vegetable stock

DIRECTIONS

1. In a saucepan heat oil over medium heat
2. Sauté the leeks for 2-3 minutes and add garlic
3. Add the rest of the ingredients and bring to boil
4. Lover the heat and simmer for another 15-20 minutes
5. Remove and serve

COCONUT SMOOTHIE

Serves: 2
Prep Time: 5 Minutes
Cook Time: 10 Minutes
Total Time: 15 Minutes

INGREDIENTS

- 1 cup coconut milk
- ¼ cup raspberries
- 1 tsp honey
- ¼ cup ice
- ¼ cup pomegranate
- ¼ cup blueberries

DIRECTIONS

1. In a blender add all the ingredients and blend until smooth
2. Pour into a glass and serve

ALMOND BUTTER

Serves: 2

Prep Time: 10 Minutes

Cook Time: 10 Minutes

Total Time: 20 Minutes

INGREDIENTS

- 1 cup roasted almonds
- ¼ tsp salt

DIRECTIONS

1. **In a blender place the ingredients and blend until smooth**
2. **Remove and serve**

BROILED FLOUNDER

Serves: **4**

Prep Time: **10** Minutes

Cook Time: **20** Minutes

Total Time: **30** Minutes

INGREDIENTS

- 1 lbs. flounder filet
- 1 tablespoon chopped shallots
- 1 clove garlic
- ¼ tsp chopped oregano
- parsley
- ½ tsp salt
- ½ cup mayonnaise
- 1 tsp mustard

DIRECTIONS

1. Preheat oven to broil
2. Mix all the ingredients (without parsley) and spread the mixture over the fish
3. Broil the fish for 10-12 minutes or until golden brown
4. Garnish with parsley and serve

CINNAMON APPLESAUCE

Serves: 2
Prep Time: 10 Minutes
Cook Time: 20 Minutes
Total Time: 30 Minutes

INGREDIENTS

- 2 lbs. green apples
- ¼ tsp salt
- 2 tsp honey
- 2/3 cup water
- ½ tsp cinnamon

DIRECTIONS

1. In a saucepan mix all the ingredients and bring to boil over medium heat
2. Cover the pot and lower the temperature
3. Cook for 20-25 minutes
4. Remove from heat and let it cool for 10-15 minutes
5. Stir in the honey and serve

SHREDDED CARROT SALAD

Serves: **4**

Prep Time: **10** Minutes

Cook Time: **30** Minutes

Total Time: **40** Minutes

INGREDIENTS

- 2 cups shredded carrots
- ¼ tsp lemon thyme
- 1 tsp apple cider vinegar
- 1 tablespoon walnuts
- ½ cup mayonnaise
- 1 tsp honey
- 1 tsp chopped chives

DIRECTIONS

1. In a bowl mix all the ingredients
2. Refrigerate for 40-50 minutes, remove and serve

MOROCCAN SALMON

Serves: 2

Prep Time: 10 Minutes

Cook Time: 20 Minutes

Total Time: 30 Minutes

INGREDIENTS

RUB
- 1 tsp garlic powder
- ½ tsp oregano
- ½ tsp curry powder
- ¼ tsp ginger
- ½ tsp onion powder
- ½ tsp ground turmeric
- ½ tsp salt

FISH
- 2 salmon filets
- 1 small onion
- 1 tablespoon olive oil

DIRECTIONS

1. **Preheat oven to 425 F**

2. In a bowl mix all the ingredients for the rub and spread it over the salmon
3. Cook the fish for 10 minutes
4. Sauté the onion in the oil and place the sautéed onion
5. Remove and serve

GRILLED SALMON WITH HERB VINAIGRETTE

Serves: **2**

Prep Time: **10** Minutes

Cook Time: **20** Minutes

Total Time: **30** Minutes

INGREDIENTS

SALMON
- 2 salmon filets
- 1 tsp olive oil
- salt
- pepper

GREENS
- 1 cup greens
- ½ cup chopped celery
- ¼ cup string beans
- 1 asparagus spears
- 1 tablespoon chopped nuts
- ½ cup shredded carrots
- 1 tablespoon dried cranberries

DIRECTIONS

1. **Preheat the oven to broil**

2. Brush the salmon filets with oil and season with salt
3. Broil the filets for 10 minutes
4. Mix all the ingredients for greens and pour ½ the vinaigrette over the greens
5. Plate the greens with grilled filet
6. Drizzle vinaigrette over the fish and serve

DINNER

BAKED ZUCCHINI

Serves: **4**

Prep Time: **10** Minutes

Cook Time: **20** Minutes

Total Time: **30** Minutes

INGREDIENTS

- 2 medium zucchini
- 2 cup shredded mozzarella cheese
- salt

DIRECTIONS

1. Slice zucchini into small pieces
2. Place flat into a cookie sheet
3. Sprinkle with salt
4. Bake for 15 minutes at 325 F
5. Remove ad sprinkle with cheese
6. Put it back in the oven for another 5 minutes
7. Remove and serve

GREEN CHILE RICE

Serves: *4*

Prep Time: *10* Minutes

Cook Time: *60* Minutes

Total Time: *70* Minutes

INGREDIENTS

- 2 cups rice
- 3 cups chicken broth
- 1 tablespoon lime juice
- 2 4 oz. cans green chiles
- 1/3 cup cilantro
- 1 tsp oregano
- 1 tsp cumin
- 3 green onions

DIRECTIONS

1. In a pan mix all the ingredients
2. Bake until rice is done at 325 F
3. Remove and serve

PESTO

Serves: **4**

Prep Time: **10** Minutes

Cook Time: **10** Minutes

Total Time: **40** Minutes

INGREDIENTS

- 2 cups basil leaves
- 1 tsp olive oil
- ½ cup parmesan cheese
- ½ tsp salt
- ½ tsp ground pepper
- ½ cup walnuts

DIRECTIONS

1. Place all the ingredients in a blender and blend until smooth
2. Add olive oil in the pesto until is the right consistency
3. Remove and serve

SWEET TOMATO RELISH

Serves: *4*

Prep Time: *10* Minutes

Cook Time: *15* Minutes

Total Time: *25* Minutes

INGREDIENTS

- 2 cups cherry tomatoes
- ½ cup dried thyme
- 2 tablespoons olive oil
- ½ cup sweet onion
- ½ cup brown sugar

DIRECTIONS

1. In a pan heat olive oil and add onions
2. Sauce for 2-3 minutes and add tomatoes, thyme and sugar
3. Smash the tomatoes with a spoon
4. When ready remove from heat and serve

MACARONI AND CHEESE

Serves: **4**

Prep Time: **20** Minutes

Cook Time: **30** Minutes

Total Time: **50** Minutes

INGREDIENTS

- 5 tablespoons butter
- 1 tsp salt
- 1 cup jake cheese
- 1 cup gruyere cheese
- ½ cup breadcrumbs
- 2 tablespoons parmesan cheese
- 2 cups macaroni dry
- ¼ cup purpose flour
- 2 cups milk
- ¼ tsp oregano
- 1 pinch red pepper

DIRECTIONS

1. **Preheat oven to 375 F**
2. **Boil a large pot of water and cook until ready**
3. **In a pan melt butter and add flour and whisk to combine**

4. Add milk and stir until smooth
5. Add seasoning and cheese and cook until each cheese is melted
6. Add pasta into the mixture
7. Sprinkle parmesan over top of pasta and serve

ROASTED BRUSEELS SPROUTS

Serves: **4**

Prep Time: **10** Minutes

Cook Time: **10** Minutes

Total Time: **20** Minutes

INGREDIENTS

- 2 tablespoons olive oil
- 1 lb. Brussels sprouts
- ½ tsp salt
- ¼ tsp black pepper
- 2 tablespoons butter
- 1 tablespoon maple syrup

DIRECTIONS

1. Preheat oven to 400 F
2. Coat Brussels sprouts with olive oil and salt
3. Pour sprouts onto baking sheet and roast for 12-15 minutes
4. Flip them while roasting
5. In a saucepan melt butter and cook until brown
6. Remove from heat and add maple syrup

CARAMELIZED ONION AND BACON

Serves: **4**

Prep Time: **10** Minutes

Cook Time: **30** Minutes

Total Time: **40** Minutes

INGREDIENTS

- 1 lbs. green beans
- 4 slices bacon
- 1 onion
- 1 tsp sugar
- 3 tablespoons butter
- salt

DIRECTIONS

1. In a pan add butter and cook onion until brown
2. Add sugar, balsamic vinegar and stir to combine
3. Transfer onions to a bowl and melt butter and add beans
4. Cook until brown for 9-10 minutes
5. Add in caramelized onions, bacon and salt

CORNCAKE

Serves: **4**

Prep Time: **10** Minutes

Cook Time: **20** Minutes

Total Time: **30** Minutes

INGREDIENTS

- ½ cup butter
- ½ cup sugar
- 1 tablespoon whipping cream
- 1/3 tssp salt
- ½ tsp baking powder
- ½ cup masa harina
- 1/3 cup water
- 1 cup creamed corn
- ½ cup corn

DIRECTIONS

1. Preheat oven to 325 F
2. Beat butter until creamy and add water and masa harina and mix
3. Add cornmeal, sugar, corn, baking powder and salt
4. Pour the mixture into an iron pan
5. Bake for 20-25 minutes, remove and serve

TERIYAKI BURGER

Serves: *4*

Prep Time: *10* Minutes

Cook Time: *20* Minutes

Total Time: *30* Minutes

INGREDIENTS

- 1 lbs. ground beep
- 2 tablespoons teriyaki sauce
- 1 tablespoon honey
- 1 tsp salt
- ¾ tsp ginger
- 1 clove garlic minced
- 4 hamburger buns
- lettuce leaves
- tomato slices

DIRECTIONS

1. Mix first 6 ingredients into 4 patties
2. Cook patties on grill
3. Place on bun, lettuce, tomato and condiments
4. Serve when ready

BBQ CHICKEN SALAD

Serves: 2

Prep Time: 5 Minutes

Cook Time: 5 Minutes

Total Time: 10 Minutes

INGREDIENTS

- 1 chicken breast
- ¼ cup dressing
- ½ cup bbq sauce
- 1 cup tortilla strips
- ½ cup bbq sauce
- 5 cups romaine lettuce
- 1 cup corn
- 1 cup black beans
- ½ cup cheese
- 1 tomato
- 1 avocado

DIRECTIONS

1. Cook the chicken and cover with bbq sauce
2. Mix corn, black beans, romaine lettuce, avocado, cheese and tomato
3. Mix together bbq sauce and dressing and add to salad

4. Serve when ready

STRAWBERRY SALAD

Serves: 2

Prep Time: 5   Minutes

Cook Time: 5   Minutes

Total Time: 10   Minutes

INGREDIENTS

- ½ lb. romaine lettuce
- ½ cup pneapple
- ½ cup strawberries
- ½ cup blueberries
- 1 can oranges
- ½ cup pecans
-

DIRECTIONS

1. Slice fruit and mix with lettuce and serve

CHICKEN PASTA SALAD

Serves: **2**

Prep Time: **5** Minutes

Cook Time: **10** Minutes

Total Time: **15** Minutes

INGREDIENTS

- 4 strips bacon
- ½ cup tomatoes
- ½ cup mayonnaise
- 3 tablespoons balsamic vinegar
- 3 onions
- 1 lb. tube pasta
- 1 lb. chicken cooked and shredded
- 3 cups spinach

DIRECTIONS

1. In a bowl add balsamic vinegar and mayonnaise and whisk well
2. In another bowl mix onion, pasta, bacon, chicken spinach and tomatoes
3. Add mayonnaise mixture and toss to combine

SPINACH PASTA SALAD

Serves: 2

Prep Time: 10 Minutes

Cook Time: 60 Minutes

Total Time: 70 Minutes

INGREDIENTS

- 6 oz. bow tie pasta

DRESSING

- 1 cup oil
- 1/3 cup teriyaki sauce
- 1 5 oz. can water chestnuts
- 2 onions
- ¼ tsp salt
- ¼ tsp pepper
- 8 oz. spinach
- 1 cup craisins
- 1 11 oz can oranges
- 2 tablespoons sesame seeds
- 1 cup peanuts
- 1/3 cup white vinegar
- 5 tablespoons sugar

DIRECTIONS

1. In a blender add all the dressing ingredients and blend
2. Combine remaining dressing and pasta and marinade for 1-2 hours
3. Add pasta and liquid and toss well
4. Remove and serve

BUTTERNUT SQUASH SOUP

Serves: **4**

Prep Time: **10** Minutes

Cook Time: **30** Minutes

Total Time: **40** Minutes

INGREDIENTS

- 2 tablespoons butter
- 24 oz. cubed butternut squash
- 2 cups chicken broth
- 1 pinch cumin
- salt
- ¼ onion
- 1 clove garlic
- ¼ tsp thyme

DIRECTIONS

1. Coat squash with olive oil and place it on a baking sheet
2. Broil for 10-12 minutes
3. In a pan melt butter and add onion, garlic and thyme
4. Add squash and chicken broth and cook for 10-12 minutes
5. Add pepper, salt and cumin
6. Remove from heat and puree the mixture

TACO SOUP

Serves: **2**

Prep Time: **10** Minutes

Cook Time: **30** Minutes

Total Time: **40** Minutes

INGREDIENTS

- 1 lb. hamburger
- 1 16 oz. can tomato sauce
- 2 16 oz. can red kidney beans
- taco seasoning
- ½ cup onion
- 3 cups water
- 2 26 oz. cans tomatoes

DIRECTIONS

1. **Combine all ingredients and simmer for 15-20 minutes**
2. **Top with cheese and sliced olives**

PUMPKIN CHILI

Serves: 2
Prep Time: **10** Minutes
Cook Time: **30** Minutes
Total Time: **40** Minutes

INGREDIENTS

- 2 tablespoons olive oil
- 1 small onion
- 2 cups chicken stock
- 1 tablespoon chili powder
- 1 tsp cumin
- ½ tsp salt
- 1 can kidney beans
- 1 green bell pepper
- 1 jalapeno seed
- 1 clove garlic
- 1 lb. ground chicken
- 1 can 15 oz. tomatoes
- 1 15 oz. can pumpkin puree

DIRECTIONS

1. In a pot heat oil and add pepper, onion and garlic
2. Sauté until tender and add turkey, pumpkin, tomatoes, chili powder, cumin and salt
3. Reduce heat and add beans
4. Simmer for 30 minutes
5. Remove from heat and serve

CHICKEN PIE SOUP

Serves: **4**

Prep Time: **10** Minutes

Cook Time: **240** Minutes

Total Time: **250** Minutes

INGREDIENTS

- 1 lb. chicken breast
- ¼ tsp pepper
- 1 cup frozen peas
- 1 cup frozen corn
- ½ tsp thyme
- 3 cups chicken broth
- ½ cup flour
- 1 tsp garlic minced
- 1 tsp salt
- 1 tsp oregano
- ½ cup onion
- 1 cup carrots

DIRECTIONS

1. In a slow cooker add all the ingredients except the peas

2. Cook for 4 hours or until chicken is ready
3. Remove chicken and shred and return to the cooker with the peas and cook for another 30 minutes
4. Use a cookie cutter and cut shapes from the pie crust
5. Bake according to directions on package and use them to garnish the soup

TOMATO TORTELLINI SOUP

Serves: **4**

Prep Time: **10** Minutes

Cook Time: **20** Minutes

Total Time: **30** Minutes

INGREDIENTS

- ½ cup chopped tomatoes
- 6 oz. cheese tortellini
- ½ cup onion
- 1 cup carrot
- 1 tsp sugar
- ½ cup whipping cream
- Parmesan cheese
- basil
- 1 tablespoon tomato paste
- 1 tsp garlic minced
- 4 cups chicken broth
- 1 cup tomatoes
- 1 tsp salt

DIRECTIONS

1. In a pot mix tomato with oil, onion, carrots, tomato paste and garlic

2. Sauté for 3-4 minutes and add salt, pepper and chicken broth
3. Simmer for 15-17 minutes
4. Puree soup with a blender until smooth
5. Cook tortellini in boiling water and add cream to soup
6. Garnish with parmesan, basil and serve

MASHED SWEET POTATO SOUP

Serves: **4**

Prep Time: **10** Minutes

Cook Time: **20** Minutes

Total Time: **30** Minutes

INGREDIENTS

- 2 cups mashed sweet potatoes
- 1 tsp cumin
- ½ cup onion
- 1 tablespoon butter
- ½ tsp salt
- 1 tablespoon cilantro
- ¼ cup coconut milk
- 2 cups chicken broth
- ½ tsp red pepper flakes

DIRECTIONS

1. In a pan over medium heat sauté onion in butter until soft
2. Add onions into sweet potatoes and chicken broth
3. Simmer for 10-15 minutes on high heat and season with salt, cumin and red pepper
4. Add coconut milk and cook for another 5-10 minutes
5. Garnish with cilantro and serve

TURKEY SOUP

Serves: **4**

Prep Time: **10** Minutes

Cook Time: **20** Minutes

Total Time: **30** Minutes

INGREDIENTS

- 1 cup onion
- 1 tsp cumin
- 1 tsp salt
- ¼ tsp salt
- ¼ tsp pepper
- 1 15 oz. can black beans
- 1 11 oz. can whole kernel corn
- 1 10 oz. can tomatoes
- 1 tsp chili powder
- 1 tsp canola oil
- 1 tsp garlic
- 3 cups chicken broth
- 2 cups turkey chopped
- grated cheese

DIRECTIONS

1. In a pan sauce onion with garlic over medium heat

2. Add the rest of ingredients and sauté for another 2-3 minutes
3. Boil and simmer for 15-20 minutes
4. Serve with grated cheese

DESSERT

GRANOLA COOKIES

Serves: 2

Prep Time: 5 Minutes

Cook Time: 10 Minutes

Total Time: 15 Minutes

INGREDIENTS

- ¾ cup pb
- ½ cup oats
- ½ cup brown sugar
- 2 cups granola
- 3 oz chocolate
- 2/3 cup honey

DIRECTIONS

1. In a blender add granola and blend until smooth
2. Lay out a piece of wax paper
3. In a saucepan mix peanut butter, honey and brown sugar
4. Bring to boil over medium heat for 4-5 minutes
5. Turn of heat and pour over granola mixture
6. Scoop onto wax paper and top with chocolate

COCONUT OIL CHEX MIX

Serves: 2

Prep Time: 5 Minutes

Cook Time: 5 Minutes

Total Time: 10 Minutes

INGREDIENTS

- 8 cups chex cereal
- 1 cup pretzel twists
- 1 cup mixed nuts
- ¼ cup melted coconut oil
- ½ coconut amino
- 1 tsp salt

DIRECTIONS

1. In a bowl mix all the ingredients together and serve

CHOCOLATE COCONUT COOKIE

Serves: **20**

Prep Time: **10** Minutes

Cook Time: **10** Minutes

Total Time: **20** Minutes

INGREDIENTS

- ¼ cup coconut oil
- ¾ cup chocolate chips
- ¼ cup brown sugar
- 1 egg
- 1 cup shredded coconut
- 1 tsp salt
- 1 cup oats

DIRECTIONS

1. Preheat oven to 325 F and line a baking sheet with parchment paper
2. In a bowl mix eggs, coconut oil and sugar until smooth
3. Add salt, oats and coconut stir well
4. Scoop the dough and shape into a ball and place on the cookie sheet
5. Bake for 15-20 minutes
6. When ready, remove and serve

COCONUT OIL CRISPY TREATS

Serves: 4

Prep Time: 10 Minutes

Cook Time: 20 Minutes

Total Time: 30 Minutes

INGREDIENTS

- ¼ cup coconut oil
- 1 10 oz. marshmallows
- 4 cups rice cereal

DIRECTIONS

1. In a pan mix marshmallow with coconut oil over medium heat until melted
2. When mixture is smooth add rice cereal and mix
3. Pour into pan and cool for an hour
4. Remove and cut into squares

PEANUT BUTTER BALLS

Serves: **24**

Prep Time: **10** Minutes

Cook Time: **20** Minutes

Total Time: **30** Minutes

INGREDIENTS

- 1 cup peanut butter
- ¼ cup M&M's
- ¾ cup brown sugar
- 1 tablespoons maple syrup
- 1 cup oats ¼ cup M&M's
- ¼ cup chocolate chips
- ¼ cup chocolate chips
- 4 tablespoons coconut oil

DIRECTIONS

1. On the counter place a wax paper and store where you will store peanut butter balls
2. In a bowl mix brown sugar, peanut butter, coconut oil, maple syrup until smooth
3. Add oats and mix
4. Add chocolate chips and M&M's and stir well
5. Form small balls and place them on the wax paper

6. Store in the refrigerator and serve

COCONUT OIL BROWNIES

Serves: *4*

Prep Time: *10* Minutes

Cook Time: *50* Minutes

Total Time: *60* Minutes

INGREDIENTS

- 1 cup chocolate chips
- ¾ cup oat flour
- ¼ tsp salt
- ¼ cup chocolate chips
- ¾ cup coconut oil
- 1 cup raw sugar
- 3 eggs
- 1 tsp vanilla

DIRECTIONS

1. In a bowl mix coconut oil and chocolate chips and microwave for 1 minute and put aside
2. Preheat oven to 325 F and and line a baking pan with foil

3. In a bowl mix eggs and sugar until smooth and add chocolate mixture and vanilla and mix well
4. Fold in the oat flour, chocolate chips, salt and pour into the pan
5. Bake for 45-50 minutes, remove and serve

BLUEBERRY BANANA MUFFINS

Serves: **4**

Prep Time: **10** Minutes

Cook Time: **30** Minutes

Total Time: **40** Minutes

INGREDIENTS

- 2 bananas
- ½ tsp baking soda
- ½ tsp cinnamon
- ½ tsp salt
- 1 cup cassava flour
- ¾ cup blueberries
- 2 eggs
- ½ cup olive oil
- ½ cup coconut sugar

DIRECTIONS

1. Preheat oven to 325 F and line a muffin tin
2. Place wet ingredients and sugar in blender and blend until smooth
3. In a bowl mix dry ingredients and pour into blender and blend until smooth
4. Add blueberries and stir

5. Pour mixture into muffin cups
6. Bake until golden brown for 20-25 minutes
7. Remove and serve

COCONUT OIL COOKIES

Serves: *4*

Prep Time: *10* Minutes

Cook Time: *10* Minutes

Total Time: *20* Minutes

INGREDIENTS

- 3 cup oats
- 1 cup sugar
- ½ cup cocoa powder
- ¼ tsp salt
- 1 tsp vanilla
- ½ cup coconut oil
- ¼ cup peanut butter
- ¼ cup cashew milk

DIRECTIONS

1. In a saucepan mix, peanut butter, cashew milk, coconut oil, sugar, salt and cocoa powder and cook over medium heat for 4-5 minutes
2. Add vanilla and oats to mixture and cook for another 2-3 minutes
3. Scoop into a wax paper and let it cool before serving

GLUTEN FREE INSTANT POT OATMEAL

Serves: 2
Prep Time: 10 Minutes
Cook Time: 10 Minutes
Total Time: 20 Minutes

INGREDIENTS

- 2 cups gluten free oats
- 2 cups water
- 2 tablespoons coconut vinegar
- 3 cups milk
- ¼ tsp sat

DIRECTIONS

1. In a bowl mix oats, water, vinegar and cover for 24 hours
2. Add oats mixture to the instant pot and add milk and salt
3. Cook for 4-5 minutes
4. Remove and serve

BANANA BREAD COOKIES

Serves: *4*

Prep Time: *10* Minutes

Cook Time: *10* Minutes

Total Time: *20* Minutes

INGREDIENTS

- 1 cup purpose flour
- 1 tsp vanilla extract
- 1 tablespoon canola oil
- ¼ cup chocolate chips
- ¼ tsp baking soda
- 1 tsp baking powder
- ½ banana
- 1 tablespoon agave syrup
- 2 tablespoons applesauce

DIRECTIONS

1. Preheat oven to 325 F
2. In a bowl mix baking soda, baking powder and flour
3. In another bowl smash a banana and add applesauce, agave syrup, vanilla extract and canola oil
4. Add wet ingredients to the dry ingredients and mix until it forms a dough

5. Add chocolate chips and mix together
6. Scoop the dough onto parchment paper covered with baking sheets
7. Bake for 10 minutes and remove when ready

CHOCOLATE BALLS

Serves: 2

Prep Time: 10 Minutes

Cook Time: 10 Minutes

Total Time: 20 Minutes

INGREDIENTS

- 1 cup oats
- 1 tsp vanilla extract
- pinch of salt
- 3 tablespoons water
- 2 tablespoons cacao powder
- 2 tablespoons hemp seeds
- 1 tablespoon chia seeds

DIRECTIONS

1. Place the ingredients into a blender and blend until smooth
2. Add water and blend again
3. Roll into small balls and refrigerate

ORANGE CREAMSICLE BALLS

Serves: **12**

Prep Time: **10** Minutes

Cook Time: **10** Minutes

Total Time: **20** Minutes

INGREDIENTS

- ¼ cup cashew butter
- 1 cup vanilla protein powder
- ¼ cup almond flour
- 2 tablespoons orange juice

DIRECTIONS

1. In a bowl mix orange juice with cashew
2. Stir until combined completely and add protein powder and almond flour
3. Roll dough into balls and store in refrigerator

PEANUT BUTTER COCONUT BITES

Serves: **12**

Prep Time: **10** Minutes

Cook Time: **20** Minutes

Total Time: **30** Minutes

INGREDIENTS

- 1 cup oats
- ½ cup maple syrup
- ½ cup peanut butter
- ¼ cup shredded coconut
- ¼ cup hemp hearts
- ½ cup chocolate chips

DIRECTIONS

1. In a bowl add shredded coconut, hemp hears, oats and chocolate chips and whisk to combine
2. Add maple syrup and peanut butter and mix until well combined
3. Scoop a tablespoon of mixture and roll into balls and set aside
4. Repeat the process and refrigerate the balls

CARROT CAKE BITES

Serves: **12**

Prep Time: **10** Minutes

Cook Time: **30** Minutes

Total Time: **40** Minutes

INGREDIENTS

- 1 cup shredded carrots
- ½ cup oats
- ¾ cup desiccated coconut
- 1/3 cup almonds
- 2 tablespoons hemp seeds
- 1 tsp cinnamon
- 1 tsp nutmeg
- 1/3 tsp ginger
- ¼ tsp salt
- 1 tablespoon coconut oil
- 1 tsp tapioca flour
- ¼ cup vegan chocolate

DIRECTIONS

1. In a bowl put ¼ of coconut
2. In a blender add all the ingredients and blend until smooth

3. Scoop out a tablespoon of the batter and roll into a ball
4. Drizzle the chocolate on top and refrigerate

PEACH COBBLER SMOOTHIE

Serves: *1*

Prep Time: *5* Minutes

Cook Time: *5* Minutes

Total Time: *10* Minutes

INGREDIENTS

- 1 cup oat milk
- ½ cup water
- 1 cup frozen peaches
- 1 tablespoon rolled oats
- ¼ tsp vanilla extract
- ¼ tsp cinnamon
- ¼ tsp nutmeg

DIRECTIONS

1. Place all the ingredients in a blender and blend until smooth
2. Pour in a glass and serve

CHERRY COCONUT SMOOTHIE

Serves: 2
Prep Time: 10 Minutes
Cook Time: 10 Minutes
Total Time: 20 Minutes

INGREDIENTS

- 2 cups frozen blueberries
- 1 cup baby spinach
- 1 16-ounce coconut milk
- red layer
- 1 cup frozen cherries
- 1 date
- 1 tablespoon hemp seeds

DIRECTIONS

1. Place all the ingredients in a blender and blend until smooth
2. Pour in a glass and serve

COCONUT BLACKOUT SMOOTHIE

Serves: 2

Prep Time: 5 Minutes

Cook Time: 5 Minutes

Total Time: 10 Minutes

INGREDIENTS

- 1 banana
- ½ cup frozen blackberries
- ¼ cup water
- ½ cup lettuce
- ½ cup coconut milk
- 1 tablespoon chia seeds
- 2 ice cubes

DIRECTIONS

1. Place all the ingredients in a blender and blend until smooth
2. Pour in a glass and serve

CARROT TURMERIC SMOTHEI

Serves: 2

Prep Time: 5 Minutes

Cook Time: 5 Minutes

Total Time: 10 Minutes

INGREDIENTS

- 5-ounces water
- 2 tsp turmeric
- 1 tsp ginger
- ¼ tsp black pepper
- 1 cup carrots
- 1 cup pineapple
- ¼ cup cashews
- 2 fresh dates

DIRECTIONS

1. Place all the ingredients in a blender and blend until smooth
2. Pour in a glass and serve

GINGERBREAD SMOOTHIE

Serves: 2

Prep Time: 5 Minutes

Cook Time: 5 Minutes

Total Time: 10 Minutes

INGREDIENTS

- 1 cup almond milk
- ¼ tsp ginger
- ½ tsp nutmeg
- ¼ tsp cloves
- 1 frozen banana
- ½ cup rolled oats
- 2 tsp black strap molasses
- ¼ tsp cinnamon

DIRECTIONS

1. Place all the ingredients in a blender and blend until smooth
2. Pour in a glass and serve

SWEET POTATO SMOOTHIE

Serves: 2
Prep Time: 5 Minutes
Cook Time: 5 Minutes
Total Time: 10 Minutes

INGREDIENTS

- 1 cup almond milk
- ¼ tsp cinnamon
- 2 ice cubes
- 1 orange
- 1 baked potato
- ¼ tsp ginger

DIRECTIONS

1. Place all the ingredients in a blender and blend until smooth
2. Pour in a glass and serve

THANK YOU FOR READING THIS BOOK!

Made in the USA
Lexington, KY
28 May 2019